12.1.17
#2760

2|18

D0872013

TRAVEL WITH THE GREAT EXPLORERS

Explore with

Mary Kingsley

Tim Cooke

Crabtree Publishing Company
www.crabtreebooks.com

Crabtree Publishing Company
www.crabtreebooks.com

Author: Tim Cooke

Designer: Lynne Lennon

Picture Manager: Sophie Mortimer

Design Manager: Keith Davis

Editorial Director: Lindsey Lowe

Children's Publisher: Anne O'Daly

Crabtree Editorial Director: Kathy Middleton

Crabtree Editor: Petrice Custance

Proofreader: Angela Kaelberer

**Production coordinator
 and prepress technician:** Tammy McGarr

Print coordinator: Margaret Amy Salter

Written and produced for Crabtree Publishing Company
by Brown Bear Books

Photographs:
Front Cover: **Public Domain:** br; **Shutterstock:** tr, Fabian Plock cr; **Wellcome Images:** main.

Interior: Alamy: Chronicle 4, 25t, 27t, Classic Collection 2 18, Classic Collection 3 21t, Granger Historical Picture Archive 21b, Ignazuri 25b, Keasbury-Gordon Photographic Arhive 15b, Mary Evans Picture Library13t, Natural History Museum 10tl, Photostock-Israel 26, Pictorial Press Ltd. 4bc, 11, 17, 24, Print Collector 12, Bertrand Rieger/Hemis 7c, Ed Scott 16; **Getty Images:** Bettmann 15, Popperfoto 5t; **istockphoto:** 22; **Library of Congress:** 5br; **Mary Evans Picture Library:** 17t; **Public Domain:** University of Edinburgh 13c, New York Public Library 19t, W. & A. K Johnston 19b; **Shutterstock:** Alexey Fedorenko 15r, Elsa Hoffman 29t, Alexander Mazurkevich 27b, ODM 23c, Hans Wagemaker 23t, 23b; **Thinkstock:** istockphoto 6, 20; **Topfoto:** Alinari 7r, The Granger Collection 28t, World History Archive 10br; **Wellcome Images:** 28-29.
All other artwork and maps, **Brown Bear Books Ltd.**

Brown Bear Books has made every attempt to contact the copyright holders. If you have any information please contact licensing@brownbearbooks.co.uk

Library and Archives Canada Cataloguing in Publication

CIP Available at the Library and Archives Canada

Library of Congress Cataloging-in-Publication Data

Names: Cooke, Tim, 1961- author.
Title: Explore with Mary Kingsley / Tim Cooke.
Description: New York, NY : Crabtree Publishing Company, 2018. |
 Series: Travel with the great explorers | Includes index.
Identifiers: LCCN 2017028416 (print) | LCCN 2017030411 (ebook) |
 ISBN 9781427178107 (Electronic HTML) |
 ISBN 9780778739203 (reinforced library binding : alk. paper) |
 ISBN 9780778739265 (pbk. : alk. paper)
Subjects: LCSH: Kingsley, Mary Henrietta, 1862-1900--Juvenile literature. |
 Explorers--Africa, West--Biography--Juvenile literature. |
 Explorers--Great Britain--Biography--Juvenile literature. | Women explorers-
 -Africa, West--Biography--Juvenile literature. | Women explorers--Great
 Britain--Biography--Juvenile literature. | Africa, West--Discovery and
 exploration--British--Juvenile literature.
Classification: LCC DT476.23.K56 (ebook) |
 LCC DT476.23.K56 C66 2018 (print) | DDC 916.604/31092 [B] --dc23
LC record available at https://lccn.loc.gov/2017028416

Crabtree Publishing Company
www.crabtreebooks.com   1-800-387-7650

Printed in Canada/092017/PB20170719

Published in Canada
Crabtree Publishing
616 Welland Ave.
St. Catharines, ON
L2M 5V6

Published in the United States
Crabtree Publishing
PMB 59051
350 Fifth Avenue, 59th Floor
New York, New York 10118

Published in the United Kingdom
Crabtree Publishing
Maritme House
Basin Road North, Hove
BN41 1WR

Published in Australia
Crabtree Publishing
3 Charles Street
Coburg North
VIC, 3058

CONTENTS

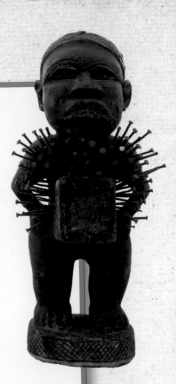

Meet the Boss

Mary Kingsley was a writer and explorer who traveled to Africa alone—unheard of for a woman at that time. Her books challenged European views of Africa, shining a light on the mistreatment of Native peoples in British colonies.

ARMCHAIR EXPLORER

+ Follows her father's travels

+ Reads about explorers

Mary Kingsley was born in 1862 in London, England. Her father, Dr. George Kingsley, spent much of Mary's childhood traveling to faraway places, including Africa. Mary longed to follow in his footsteps. She read everything she could find in her father's library. She read newspaper accounts of Henry Stanley's search for David Livingstone, and their meeting in Africa in 1871 (above).

A YOUNG NURSE

★ Mother is an invalid

★ Father gets sick, too

In 1888, Mary's mother had a stroke. Although Mary had no nursing training, she took care of her mother 24 hours a day. When her father's heart grew weak, she took care of him, too. Her father died on February 2, 1892. Her mother died just 10 weeks later.

SECOND-CLASS CITIZEN

☛ No school for girls

☛ Boys are favored

In Victorian England boys were often sent to school to be educated (right). Girls were taught at home by a governess. Mary taught herself from books such as George Craik's *Pursuit of Knowledge Under Difficulties* (1842). When Mary's brother, Charley, went to study at Cambridge University, the Kingsleys moved to Cambridge, where Mary looked after the housework.

Cambridge

When Mary moved to Cambridge, the university there had very few female students. The first colleges for women had only just opened.

INHERITANCE!

★ Mary inherits money

★ Is free to travel

When their parents died in 1892, Mary and Charles both **inherited** money from their father. Mary received an income of £500 a year (equivalent to around $55,000 today). She no longer had to worry about the future, and did not need to work for a living. She could now afford to travel.

FAMOUS UNCLE

+ Bestselling Author

Mary's uncle, her father's older brother, Charles Kingsley, was a pastor and **social reformer** as well as a famous Victorian novelist. *The Water-Babies* (1863) was one of the most popular books of the time. It told the story of Tom, a chimney sweep, who drowns and becomes a "water-baby" (left). Charles Kingsley wrote the book as part of a campaign against children being forced to work.

Where Are We Heading?

After the death of her parents, Mary planned to visit Africa to complete her father's unfinished book about the region. She prepared by visiting the Canary Islands.

Did you know ?

When Mary visited Africa in the 1890s, the continent had just become important in Europe. Different European countries wanted to claim parts of Africa to get hold of its valuable resources.

A SUBTROPICAL ISLAND

☛ **First stop**

☛ **Dramatic scenery to enjoy**

In 1892, Mary decided to travel to the Canary Islands off northwest Africa. It took a week to sail from England to the volcanic islands. Mary liked the scenery, which was more dramatic than in England (right). She stayed much longer than she planned. She often paddled between islands in a canoe.

A SIDE TRIP

+ **Exciting trip to La Gomera**

La Gomera is one of the least visited of the Canary Islands. When Mary took a trip to La Gomera, she was so busy exploring that she missed the boat back to the main island where she was staying. Mary had to spend the night sleeping under a rock on the island. It was the first of her travel adventures.

FIRST TRIP

+ Africa at last

+ Mary travels inland

Mary sailed for Africa on board the SS *Lagos* in August 1893. Every time the boat docked as it sailed along the African coast, Mary got off to explore the region. Finally, she arrived in what is now Angola (right). From there, she traveled inland. Mary spent five months traveling through the forested Congo region. She met many **Indigenous** people there.

SECOND TRIP

☞ Longs for Africa

Back in England, Mary missed Africa. In December 1894 she went back. This time, she visited the Ogooué River region (left). She traveled so far upriver that she was the first European woman to meet the Fang people. She also became the first European woman to climb Mount Cameroon. When Mary arrived back in England, reports of her journeys had made her famous.

SOUTH AFRICA

★ A Final Trip

★ Volunteers as a Nurse

In 1899, the Boer War broke out when Dutch farmers called Boers fought against the English government of South Africa. Mary volunteered to work as a military nurse, and in March 1900 she sailed back to Africa. Her work was cut short when she caught **enteric** fever. She died in South Africa on June 3, 1900.

MARY KINGLSEY'S TRAVELS IN WEST AFRICA

Mary Kingsley made two trips to West Africa. Her travels took her along the coast and inland. She traveled through the Congo and up the Ogooué River into the remote rain forest.

NIGERIA

Calabar

Mount Camere

EQUATOR
GUINEA

Libreville

Glass

Fallaba

Ogooué River

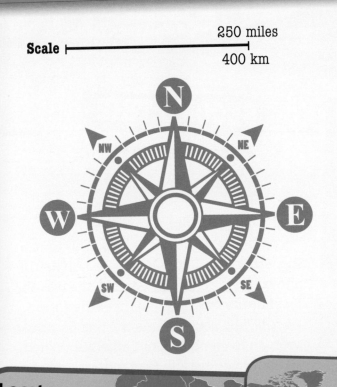

250 miles

Scale

400 km

N

NW

NE

W

E

SW

SE

S

Locator map

Africa

Luanda
Mary visited the capital of Angola on her first visit to West Africa in 1893. She used the port as a base to prepare for her expedition into the rain forest.

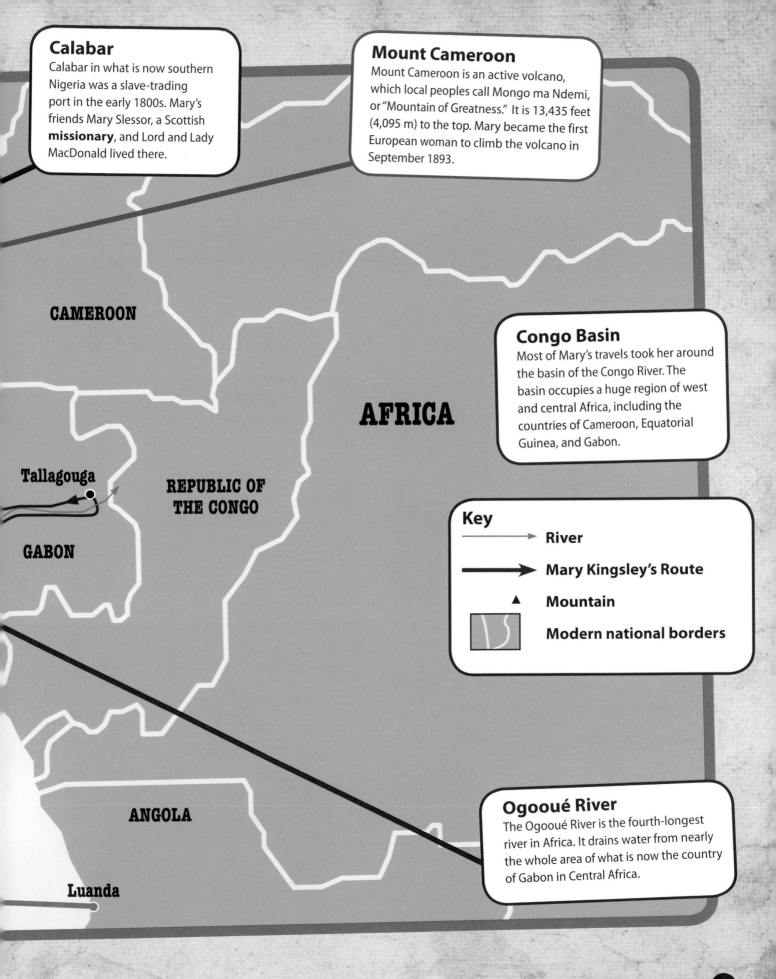

Calabar

Calabar in what is now southern Nigeria was a slave-trading port in the early 1800s. Mary's friends Mary Slessor, a Scottish **missionary**, and Lord and Lady MacDonald lived there.

Mount Cameroon

Mount Cameroon is an active volcano, which local peoples call Mongo ma Ndemi, or "Mountain of Greatness." It is 13,435 feet (4,095 m) to the top. Mary became the first European woman to climb the volcano in September 1893.

CAMEROON

Congo Basin

Most of Mary's travels took her around the basin of the Congo River. The basin occupies a huge region of west and central Africa, including the countries of Cameroon, Equatorial Guinea, and Gabon.

AFRICA

Tallagouga

REPUBLIC OF THE CONGO

GABON

Key

→ River

➡ Mary Kingsley's Route

▲ Mountain

▨ Modern national borders

ANGOLA

Ogooué River

The Ogooué River is the fourth-longest river in Africa. It drains water from nearly the whole area of what is now the country of Gabon in Central Africa.

Luanda

Meet the Crew

During her travels, Mary met and was helped by many African peoples from different tribes. She also met many Europeans, and many of them also aided in her journeys.

Native Crew

In Africa, Mary often traveled along rivers by canoe. She hired a crew of Native men to paddle the canoe and act as guides. The crew came from many different tribes, including the Fang, Ilgawa, and M'pongwe.

A LUCKY REQUEST

+ Bring back some fish!

Once she decided to travel to West Africa in 1893, Mary decided to find financial backing for her trip. She had money of her own, but hiring guides and equipment was expensive. She asked Albert Günther (left), a **naturalist** at the British Museum, if he needed any **specimens**. Günther asked Mary to bring back insects and fish. He was so impressed with what she found that he commissioned her again for her second trip.

ANOTHER MARY

- ☛ Scottish missionary in Calabar
- ☛ Lifelong friend of Kingsley

On her second trip to Africa, Mary met Mary Slessor, a Scottish missionary and teacher living in the port of Calabar in what is now Nigeria. Slessor had moved to Africa to try to **convert** people to Christianity. She learned African languages, taught local women about health care, and cared for many African children (right). Slessor and Mary Kingsley often wrote each other and remained friends throughout their lives.

A REMARKABLE MAN

☛ Expert on remote African customs

Mary met the British trader Richard Dennett in the town of Cabinda in the French Congo (present-day Gabon). Dennett lived in the town and had married a local woman. He had become an expert on the African peoples among whom he lived. He taught Mary much about the culture and customs of different tribal groups.

INFLUENTIAL FRIENDS

+ Wife becomes Mary's friend

Two people who played an important role in Mary's time in West Africa were Sir Claude MacDonald, who was an important British official, and his wife, Ethel. Lady MacDonald and Mary became friends, which allowed Mary to enjoy a taste of the MacDonalds' privileged lifestyle. Mary lived with Sir Claude and Lady MacDonald in Calabar, and the three traveled on explorations inland together.

A LATE FRIENDSHIP

★ A famous author and adventurer

★ Kipling praises Mary

When Mary traveled to South Africa in 1900, she became great friends with Rudyard Kipling (above, lying on the right). By then Kipling was a famous writer who was employed as a war correspondent to cover the Boer War. Kipling thought Mary was the bravest woman he had ever met.

Check Out the Ride

The only way to travel long distances overseas in Victorian England was by ship or train. To get to Africa, Mary sailed on steamships. In Africa, she traveled by smaller boats and railroads.

TRAVEL UPDATE

Sailing to Africa

★ The only way for travelers from Europe to reach Africa is by cargo ship. Be like Mary and try the SS *Lagos*, commanded by Captain Murray. The ship's route takes it to the Canary Islands and along the coast of West Africa. Be warned: because it is not a passenger ship, conditions on board will be cramped!

Did you know ?

West Africa has many large rivers. Some of the best known are the Niger, the Volta, and the Senegal. Mary traveled up the Ogooué River, which is 750 miles (1,200 km) long.

MOVING BY RIVER

+ Traveling by canoe

+ Look out for crocodiles!

Traveling on foot was difficult in the dense **tropical** forests of West Africa. Paths got lost in the thick vegetation. Local peoples preferred to travel by river. They carved **dugout canoes** from logs to paddle around. There were many hazards, such as **rapids** where canoes had to be carried (right). Sometimes, a hungry crocodile snatched a person from a canoe.

CANOE LIKE A LOCAL

★ **Best way to travel upstream**

★ **Rapids pose a threat**

Mary hired a dugout canoe to travel up the Ogooué River with a crew of local people (right). They passed many dangerous rapids. The crew taught Mary to paddle. Later, Mary wrote that one of the proudest achievements of her life was her ability to paddle an Ogooué canoe.

> " Being human, she must have been afraid of something, but one never found out what it was."
> *Rudyard Kipling describes Mary's bravery.*

 Weather Forecast

THRONE OF THUNDER!

If you're climbing the "Throne of Thunder," or Mount Cameroon, wrap up warm. It's cold 13,435 feet (4,095 m) in the air. There's also little oxygen above 9,850 feet (3,000 m), so you may have difficulty breathing. In September 1895, Mary took ten days to reach the summit and just two to come down. She was the first European woman to climb the mountain, and she took a route no one had taken before.

A SCARY RIDE

☞ **Congo Free State Railway**

☞ **Hairpin turns, steep descents**

The Congo Free State Railway (above) was built to carry **ivory** and rubber to the coast. Mary said that taking the railroad was "one of the most risky things you can do in all Africa." The railroad was badly laid out on narrow ridges of land above the roaring Congo River. It was not for the nervous. The year before Mary rode the train, an engine left the track and plowed into a pile of dynamite. Everyone on board died in the explosion.

EXPLORE WITH MARY KINGSLEY

Solve It With Science

Mary added to people's knowledge about the world by collecting rare species of insect and fish. She also gathered information about many cultures in Africa.

Malaria

Malaria is a disease transmitted by mosquito bites. It has killed many people in Africa. In 1820 Europeans used Indigenous knowledge to make quinine from the bark of cinchona trees. The drug helped cure malaria.

MARY THE ETHNOGRAPHER

★ Studying peoples

★ Meeting new tribes

Mary's travel writings included descriptions of different tribes she met, such as the Bubis people who lived on the island of Fernando Po, and the Fang people (above) who lived inland. Mary's descriptions of African peoples educated Europeans who knew little about West Africa at the time. She also helped to dispel many European myths about Africans, such as that the Fang were hostile **cannibals**.

 Weather Forecast

CLIMATE AND DISEASE!

West Africa was very dangerous for European visitors. It had a damp tropical climate and many insects that carried disease. Many visitors caught fatal fevers or sicknesses such as smallpox. In the late 1800s, West Africa was known as "the white man's grave."

COLLECTING SPECIMENS

+ Fish and insects

Mary's luggage on her trips included heavy glass jars and chemical preservative for specimens of fish and insects. The specimens she found on her first trip were so impressive that Albert Günther at the Natural History Museum (right) commissioned her again. This time, he asked her to bring back freshwater fish from the area between the Niger and Congo rivers. Mary returned with an unknown species of fish, a new snake, and eight new insects.

My Explorer Journal

★Imagine you were going to study medicine before making a trip to a remote location on your own. Make a list of the kind of illnesses you think it would be most useful to learn to treat.

PLANNING AHEAD

- Studies medicine in Germany
- Learns first aid

West Africa had a reputation for causing sickness. Before she went there, Mary traveled to Germany to study first aid at the famous health institute in Kaiserwerth (left). She learned how to deal with ankle sprains and snakebites. She also learned to treat malaria and yellow fever, which was another common tropical disease caused by insect bites.

Hanging at Home

Unlike most European travelers in Africa, Mary planned to eat local food and to sleep in traditional village houses—or even under the stars when she had to.

Did you know ?

In the area around Mount Cameroon, local peoples built circular huts made from dried mud. The pointed roofs were made from dried grass. The grass was layered to keep out the rain.

VILLAGE LIFE

- Huts with straw roofs
- Villagers wear few clothes

When Mary lived with local peoples in the African forests, she discovered there was little privacy. Everyone knew about each other's lives. Mary bathed in the river like the local people, and she ate local food. The people wore little clothing because it was so hot. Mary did not mind—but she continued to wear her normal clothes.

THE SPOTTED DEATH

+ Locals believe devil causes disease

When Mary visited West Africa in 1893, the region had suffered an **epidemic** of smallpox. The disease covers its victims in spots, spreads easily, and can be fatal. The Africans called it "spotted death." They believed that evil spirits or witches sent disease to people who were bad. Mary visited remote villages that were almost empty because disease had killed most of the villagers.

I'M HUNGRY

★ Food runs out

★ Starving on the mountain

On the climb up Mount Cameroon in 1895, Mary and her guides soon ran out of water. The waterholes were empty. While the guides waited for supplies, Mary carried on up the mountain despite having nothing to drink or eat. Supplies turned up the next day. The guides feasted on rice and beef. Mary enjoyed a special food box—including cookies from England!

Food Treats

In the 1890s, the British Empire stretched across the world. Many British people lived abroad. Manufacturers in Britain made goods especially to export to the empire. They sold cookies in tins, so the cookies would not get soft or broken.

> It is at these times that you realize the blessings of a good thick skirt."
> *Kingsley describes surviving the animal trap.*

SAVED BY THE SKIRT

☞ Mary falls into a trap

☞ Skirt keeps her alive!

When she was walking in the forest one day, Mary fell into an animal trap. This was a deep hole dug into the ground and covered with leaves. The bottom was full of sharp wooden stakes. The thick cloth of Mary's skirt protected her from the spikes. Many of her friends had advised Mary to wear pants while she was in Africa, but she had refused. It's a good thing she did!

Meeting and Greeting

Mary wanted to travel to West Africa because her father had studied and written about different peoples there. She wanted to finish the book he had been writing when he died.

THE SCARY FANG

- Fierce reputation
- Live in isolation

Mary trekked deep into the forest between the Ogooué and Remboué rivers with four local guides. She was the first European to travel so far inland in the region. She met the Fang people (right), who were said to be cannibals. Mary cured several sick villagers using medical techniques she had learned at the health institute in Germany. The Fang invited her to stay with them. She wrote about them in her own books.

TRAVEL UPDATE

Traveling Uniform

★ When visiting a new place, it helps to make an impression. Mary Kingsley used to walk into Fang villages dressed from head to foot in black and carrying a rolled umbrella. The Fang had seen few white men and no white women. Mary's appearance made Fang children cry with fear until their parents told them not to be scared.

Respect!

Mary had a lot of respect for the Fang people. In return, Mary was able to earn the respect of the Fang by trading with them and by caring for sick people, using skills she had learned when nursing her parents.

MAKING FRIENDS

+ Mary trades with local people

+ No women traders before

One way Mary gained the confidence of local villagers was by trading. On one trip, she bought 25 balls of rubber from chiefs of various villages. When one chief's wife admired Mary's red silk tie, she exchanged it for a necklace made from elephant hair. The villagers were more used to male European traders who provided them with fishhooks and liquor. In return, the Fang gave traders rubber and ivory (right).

Did you know ?

One reason the Fang were thought to be cannibals was because they kept human bones in boxes near their villages. Mary learned that this was how the Fang honored their dead relatives—not because they ate people!

THE SCRAMBLE FOR AFRICA

★ Europe claims African land

★ Mary disagrees

Mary visited Africa in the 1890s, the peak of a time called "the scramble for Africa." Different European powers wanted land in Africa for the natural resources, such as rubber. Europeans defended taking African land by claiming that the local people were "**savages**." Mary strongly disagreed with this view. She admired African peoples and attempted to change European views on Africans through her writings and lectures.

Learning About Africa

After her first journey to Africa, Mary wrote *Travels in West Africa*. The book was the first time many African peoples had been written about.

Pressure

Many Europeans in Africa tried to change traditional African society. They tried to force Native peoples to give up traditional practices such as having large extended families.

PEOPLES OF WEST AFRICA

☞ Many peoples live in the forests

☞ Mary meets them all

The forests of West Africa were home to many different peoples. They spoke different languages and had their own beliefs. Mary met the Bubi, the Igbo, and the Adjoumba. Many of the tribes had suffered devastating losses when Europeans first arrived in the 1500s. The explorers brought diseases with them that had never been seen in Africa before.

FETISHISM

★ Sacred objects

★ Important rituals

Europeans used the name fetishism to describe the religious practices they found in West Africa. Fetishism is the worship of objects. Any kind of object could be a fetish. Fetishes included the bones of ancestors or statues carved out of wood or studded with nails (right). As Mary learned more about African peoples, she realized that they did not simply worship objects. The objects were just one part of a more complex system of beliefs.

"CAPTAIN JOHNSON"

- ☛ Local trader
- ☛ Travels with Mary

Mary met the trader Obanjo on the Remboué River. Obanjo liked to be called Captain Johnson, but nobody knew why. The odd couple set off together in an old boat. Two Fang boys persuaded Captain Johnson to take them on board without telling their parents. The mother of one of the boys chased them down the river in her canoe. A group of armed Fang men in another canoe joined the chase! The Fang boys returned home.

My Explorer Journal

★ Imagine you are going to live in a different country. Would you try to live like local people, as Mary did? Or would you prefer to continue living as you do at home, like many of her friends? Give reasons for your answer.

Did you know ?

Mary disagreed with the way many Europeans treated the African peoples. She wondered why missionaries wanted to force Native peoples to change their religion. She saw traditional religions as a basis for strong communities.

TRAVEL UPDATE

Living the European Way

★ Why bother going to Africa to live like you're in Europe? Mary helped her friend, Lady Ethel MacDonald (left), with her official duties. Mary noticed that many European women in Africa lived like they had at home, and did not learn local customs or try local food. Mary did not approve.

I Love Nature

Mary wrote that she felt she belonged more to nature than to humankind. She loved the coasts, forests, mangrove swamps, and rivers of West Africa.

Close Call

In the jungle, Mary and two Fang hunters were once attacked by an angry male gorilla. The hunters waited while the gorilla charged forward. One of them shot it with his rifle when it was only inches away.

LEOPARD ATTACK!

+ Mary fights off a leopard

Mary was staying in a trader's house in the forest one night when she heard a dog growling. Out on the porch, a large black leopard (right) had leapt on the dog and was fighting with it. Thinking quickly, Mary threw a chair at the leopard. The big cat turned to attack her. She threw a bowl, hitting the animal on the head. The leopard finally slunk off into the night.

LET'S GO FISHING!

★ Mary collects new fish

Fishing was an important part of Mary's travels. She wanted to collect species that would impress Albert Günther in London. Once while fishing, Mary got stuck in stinking black mud at the side of the river. While washing off her skirt, she was startled to see four heads that seemed to be floating in the mud. The heads actually belonged to men who were submerged in the river mud, trying to catch fish with their bare hands.

SUNSHINE MEANS DANGER

The West African sun makes life hot for travelers—and for animals. More than once on the river, Mary came across crocodiles sunbathing on rocks. Crocodiles sometimes snatched people from their canoes. Mary wrote that she would rather watch them from the safety of a steamer than from her canoe!

INTO THE WOODS

- Dense rain forest
- Mary learns its secrets

Mary found the African rain forest a mystery until she grew used to it. She learned to identify the many different plants, from the gigantic trees to the climbing grasses and flowering **creepers**. She learned which plants were used for food and medicine and which were harmful. Local guides helped teach her to spot snakes, beetles, and bats that at first she did not even notice.

OUT OF THE WAY!

★ **Timid hippos**

Hippopotamuses were common in West Africa. They sometimes wandered into villages looking for food. Although the animals can be extremely dangerous, Mary found them to be timid. Once when she found a hippo blocking her path, she prodded it with the tip of her rolled umbrella. The animal ran off.

Fortune Hunting

Before she went to Africa, Mary spent many years looking after her family and learned to be careful with money. She took those skills with her to Africa!

AN INHERITANCE

★ Mary and Charley both inherit

★ First time Mary has money

On their parents' deaths in 1892, Mary and Charley (right, with his wife) inherited equal amounts of money. Mary could afford to fulfill her dream of traveling. Charley was not good with money. He spent most of his inheritance. When Mary came back from Africa in 1894, she had to make money to provide for them both.

A FAMOUS AUTHOR

+ Mary keeps detailed diary

Back in England after her second trip, Mary missed Africa so much she decided to write about her experiences. When *Travels in West Africa* was published in 1897, it caused a sensation. Nobody could believe that Mary had done so many amazing things in a country where no women traveled on their own. The book made Mary a wealthy woman.

TRADING FOR PROFIT

★ Africa's rich resources

Mary knew it would be easier to meet tribes such as the Fang if she took goods to trade with them. African peoples were eager to get hold of practical goods, such as fishhooks. The Europeans exchanged them for resources such as rubber and ivory. European traders gathered in bases called factories (below). Mary even traded her own clothes and jewelry!

My Explorer Journal

★ Imagine you are heading into the jungle to meet peoples who had met few outsiders. What sort of items would you take to trade that they might like, and why?

GET SOME FISH!

- ☛ Paid to collect specimens
- ☛ Goes back for more

When Mary sailed to West Africa in 1893, the British Museum of Natural History was only 12 years old. Dr. Albert Günther wanted to increase the zoology collection (left), so he asked Mary to find new specimens of fish and insects. Mary was pleased to have been asked to do such an important task. Some species Mary collected were unknown outside Africa. One was named after her, *Ctenopoma Kingsleyae*.

This Isn't What It Said in the Brochure!

Before Mary wrote *Travels in West Africa*, the only people who knew anything about the area were missionaries and traders. Mary did not know what would happen—but she still went to the region.

WILL I GET EATEN?

- Terrifying stories
- Mary unafraid

When Mary arrived in West Africa, Europeans living in towns there told her that the Fang (right) were cannibals. That made Mary eager to meet them to see if they lived up to their scary reputation. In fact, the Fang were so friendly they let Mary stay in their villages in exchange for her medical supplies and nursing skills.

STAYING HEALTHY

★ Only gets sick at home

Despite the different fevers that killed many travelers to Africa, Mary stayed healthy in Africa. She got used to blood-sucking **leeches**, fleas, and mosquitoes, and was never seriously sick during her travels. She only got very sick when she returned to England. Some people think that is because she was so happy in Africa and unhappy when back in England.

Mary spent time in African towns while she prepared for her expeditions into the forest. She was shocked by the way other Europeans tried to make their lives in Africa the same as the lives they had left in Europe. She visited Christianborg Castle in Accra, Ghana. Mary could not believe anyone had built a Danish-style castle in Africa (right). Everyone lived in the castle just as though they were back at home in Europe. They gathered for tea in the afternoon and got dressed up for dinner, despite the heat!

Mangroves

Mangrove trees grow in tidal swamps along tropical coasts. The trees have thick, tangled roots that grow above the ground. The roots grow so thickly they block routes through the swamp.

TRAVEL UPDATE

Get Out and Walk

★ If your river journey is blocked by a mangrove swamp, there is only one thing to do. Get out of your canoe and clamber through the mangrove roots to reach the other side of the swamp. You'll have to wade through deep water. There may be swarms of mangrove flies. The swamp also stinks. Even Mary Kingsley found crossing mangrove swamps an ordeal!

End of the Road

Legacy

Mary's writings and lectures educated Britons about Africa. She influenced some people to take action. These people campaigned for better treatment for African peoples in British colonies.

Mary's African adventures began when she was 30 years old. By the age of 37, she was dead. Mary had experienced and accomplished much in only seven years.

UNHAPPY AT HOME

☛ **Mary returns home**

☛ **But misses Africa**

Mary returned to a cold English winter in January 1894. She wanted to go back to Africa, but she spent most of the year looking after her brother, Charley, who was sick. Mary also had to take care of him financially, because he had spent nearly all his inheritance. Mary missed Africa, but was reluctant to leave Charley. In the end, she decided to make a second trip to Africa in 1895.

A TRIUMPHANT RETURN

★ **Travel makes Mary famous**

After Mary's second trip to Africa, she became a celebrity. Her book was published in 1897, and she spent the next three years giving lectures about her experiences in Africa. Mary also wrote to government officials to complain about how the British government behaved toward Africans. She felt strongly that Africans were being badly treated, such as being forced to pay unfair taxes.

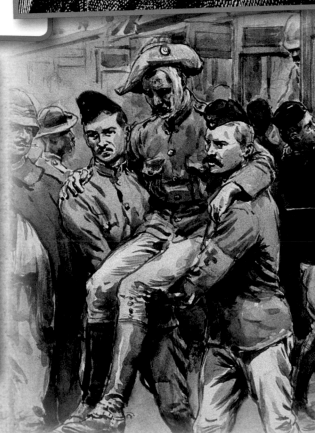

FINAL TRIP TO AFRICA

+ Boer War breaks out

In March 1900, Mary sailed for South Africa (above). The ship was full of British soldiers heading to fight in the Boer War. Many of the men got sick, and Mary spent the voyage looking after them. When she arrived in Cape Town, she worked in a hospital for wounded Boer soldiers (below) in nearby Simonstown. Many of the soldiers had **typhoid**, and the hospital was dirty and full of **lice** and bugs.

DEATH FROM FEVER

★ **Explorer falls sick**

★ **Buried at sea**

Only weeks after Mary arrived in South Africa, she caught enteric fever. Within a few days, it was clear she was going to die. On June 3, 1900, Mary Kingsley died in her sleep at just 37 years old. As she had requested, Mary was buried at sea off the coast of her beloved Africa.

LASTING LEGACY

☛ **Mary reveals the facts**

☛ **And makes a difference**

Through her work, Mary had shown Europeans how African society was organized. She also made people aware that African peoples were often treated unfairly in Britain's colonies. Her work encouraged people to found the Fair Commerce Party, which campaigned for better conditions for African peoples throughout the British Empire. Mary's exploration and her work collecting scientific specimens also challenged Victorian ideas that such tasks could only be done by men.

GLOSSARY

cannibals People who eat other people

colonies Regions in one country that are governed by another country

convert To persuade someone to change one religion for another

creepers Plants that grow along the ground or around other plants

dugout canoes Canoes made by hollowing out single logs

enteric Relating to the intestines, which are part of the digestive system

epidemic A severe outbreak of an infectious disease in a community

ethnographer Someone who studies people and culture in an organized, scientific way

governess A woman employed to teach children in their own home

Indigenous Describes people who originally came from a particular region

inherited Received money or possessions left by someone who has died

ivory A hard, creamy-white substance obtained from animal tusks

leeches Wormlike parasites that become attached to human or animal skin to suck blood

lice Small insects that live as parasites on human or animal skin

malaria A serious fever caused by mosquitoes

missionary A person who promotes a religion in a foreign country

naturalist A scientist who studies plants and animals

rapids A fast-flowing, rocky stretch of a river

resources Substances that have a use or value, such as oil or rubber

savages A negative word for people who are considered to be uncivilized

social reformer Someone who campaigns for improvements to benefit certain parts of society, such as the conditions of the poor

specimens Individual plants or animals that are studied as examples of their species or type

tropical From the hot and humid regions on either side of the equator

typhoid A severe infectious fever caused by bacteria

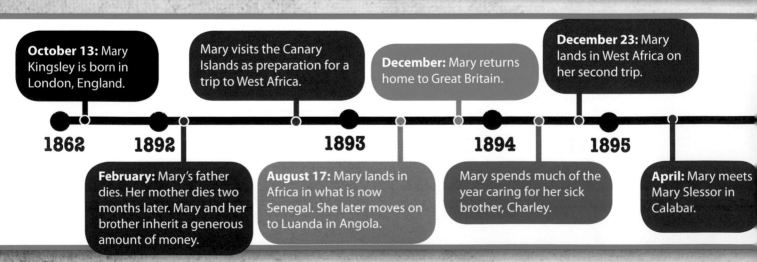

October 13: Mary Kingsley is born in London, England.

Mary visits the Canary Islands as preparation for a trip to West Africa.

December: Mary returns home to Great Britain.

December 23: Mary lands in West Africa on her second trip.

1862   **1892**   **1893**   **1894**   **1895**

February: Mary's father dies. Her mother dies two months later. Mary and her brother inherit a generous amount of money.

August 17: Mary lands in Africa in what is now Senegal. She later moves on to Luanda in Angola.

Mary spends much of the year caring for her sick brother, Charley.

April: Mary meets Mary Slessor in Calabar.

ON THE WEB

www.victorianweb.org/history/explorers/1.html
An article from the Victorian Website about the importance of Mary's explorations in Africa.

www.enchantedlearning.com/explorers/page/k/kingsley.shtml
A biography of Mary Kingsley aimed at young readers.

spartacus-educational.com/Wkingsley.htm
A biography of Mary Kingsley from Spartacus Educational.

womenineuropeanhistory.org/index.php?title=Mary_Kingsley
This site considers what Mary's life reveals about the history of women in the 1800s.

www.nonfictionminute.com/the-nonfiction-minute/mary-kingsley
An illustrated blog about Mary Kingsley from the illustrator and writer Roxie Munro.

www.newworldencyclopedia.org/entry/Mary_Henrietta_Kingsley
New World Encyclopedia entry on Mary Kingsley, with a timeline.

BOOKS

Brown, Don. *Uncommon Traveler: Mary Kingsley in Africa*. Houghton Mifflin, 2003.

Frank, Katherine. *A Voyager Out: The Life of Mary Kingsley*. Tauris Parke Paperbacks, 2005.

Kingsley, Mary H. *Travels in West Africa*. National Geographic Books, 2002.

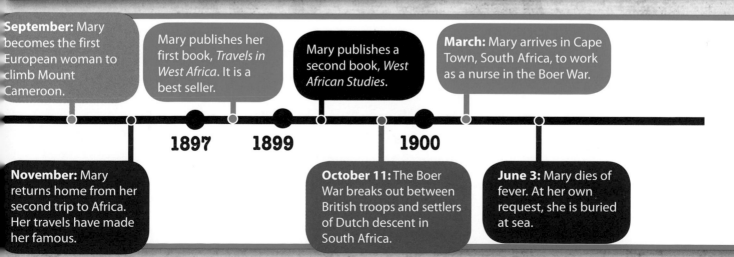

September: Mary becomes the first European woman to climb Mount Cameroon.

Mary publishes her first book, *Travels in West Africa*. It is a best seller.

Mary publishes a second book, *West African Studies*.

March: Mary arrives in Cape Town, South Africa, to work as a nurse in the Boer War.

1897

1899

1900

November: Mary returns home from her second trip to Africa. Her travels have made her famous.

October 11: The Boer War breaks out between British troops and settlers of Dutch descent in South Africa.

June 3: Mary dies of fever. At her own request, she is buried at sea.

INDEX